Fish

ANIMAL FACTS

by Heather C. Hudak

WEIGL PUBLISHERS INC.

Published by Weigl Publishers Inc.
350 5th Avenue, Suite 3304, PMB 6G
New York, NY 10118-0069 USA
Web site: www.weigl.com

Library of Congress Cataloging-in-Publication Data

Hudak, Heather C., 1975-
  Fish / Heather C. Hudak.
      p. cm. -- (Animal facts)
  Includes index.
  ISBN 1-59036-202-0 (library binding : alk. paper) 1-59036-243-8 (softcover)
  1. Fishes--Juvenile literature. I. Title.
  QL617.2.H83 2004
  591.77--dc22
                                    2004002975

Printed in the United States of America
1 2 3 4 5 6 7 8 9 0   08 07 06 05 04

Project Coordinator Heather C. Hudak   **Substantive Editor** Donald Wells
Copy Editor Janice L. Redlin   **Design** Janine Vangool   **Layout** Bryan Pezzi
Photo Researcher Ellen Bryan

Photograph and Text Credits
Every reasonable effort has been made to trace ownership and to obtain
permission to reprint copyright material. The publishers would be pleased
to have any errors or omissions brought to their attention so that they may
be corrected in subsequent printings.

Cover: Photos.com; **Corel Corporation:** page 21; **Digital Stock:** pages 3, 7B, 8, 14T,
16/17, 19L, 22, 23; **DigitalVision:** page 18; **Aaron Norman Photography:** pages 4, 5,
7T, 7M, 9R, 12, 15B, 17T, 17B, 19R; **Photos.com:** pages 1, 6, 9L, 13, 20; **Tom Stack &
Associates:** pages 10 (Tom & Therisa Stack), 11L (Tom & Therisa Stack), 11R (Tom &
Therisa Stack), 15T (David Fleetham); **©2004 Norbert Wu/www.norbertwu.com:**
page 14B.

All of the Internet URLs given in the book were valid at the time of publication.
However, due to the dynamic nature of the Internet, some addresses may have
changed, or sites may have ceased to exist since publication. While the author
and publisher regret any inconvenience this may cause readers, no responsibility
for any such changes can be accepted by either the author or the publisher.

Contents

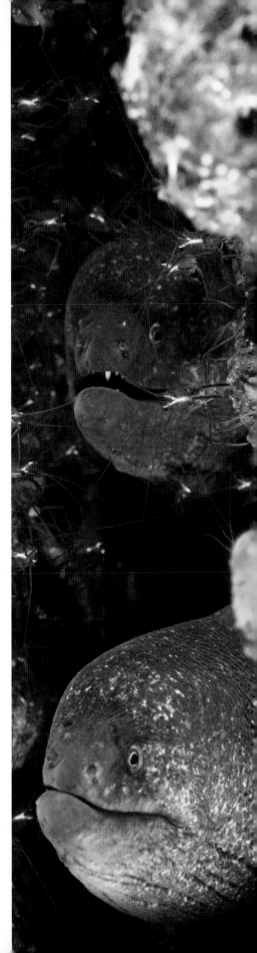

What Is a Fish?

Piranhas are scavengers. This means they feed on dead animals. Piranhas travel in large schools.

The pygmy goby is found in the streams and lakes of the Philippines.

Fish live in the water. Some fish live in hot tropical waters. Others live in very cold arctic waters. Fish live in rivers, oceans, lakes, and streams. All fish have gills. Fish use their gills to breathe under water. Most fish have fins. Fish have vertebrae, too. This means they have a backbone, or spine. Almost all fish are cold-blooded animals. This means they cannot heat their bodies. A fish's body is the same temperature as the water in which it lives.

Fish come in all shapes and sizes. Some fish are very small. Others are very large. Fish can be round or flat. They can be many colors, too.

Fish have lived on Earth for more than 500 million years. Today, there are more than 25,000 fish **species**. Each fish has special features. These features help them survive in different **habitats** and climates, or temperatures.

Fast Facts

The smallest fish is the pygmy goby. It is only 0.5 inches (13 millimeters) long. The largest fish is the whale shark. It can be 60 feet (18 meters) long.

There are more fish species than all other land and water vertebrates together.

Fish need to rest. Some fish sleep. Others do not move for a period of time. They may still move their fins. This allows them to stay in one place.

About 20 percent of fish live in groups. These groups are called schools.

Familiar Fish

There are two main groups of fish. These groups are jawed and jawless. There are two types of jawless fish. These are the hagfish and the lampreys. There are two types of jawed fish, too. These are the bony fish and the cartilaginous fish. Many types of fish are not well known. Some live deep in the ocean. Others live in jungle waters or coral reefs. Coral reefs are the hard skeletons of many tiny sea animals.

Yellowtail fish do not swim in large schools like many other ocean fish. Their schools may only have 50 to 200 fish.

Hagfish and lampreys make up less than one percent of all fish species. Jawless fish have toothed tongues. They have circular mouths with rows of horny teeth. Only a few of these fish live today. Hagfish and lampreys are snakelike fish. The brook lamprey, pictured left, belongs to this group.

Bony fish have bone skeletons. There are about 24,000 bony fish species. Bony fish live in almost all types of water. Goldfish, pictured left, salmon, and eels are bony fish.

Cartilaginous fish have cartilage skeletons. Cartilage is a tough, stretchy tissue. There are about 1,000 cartilaginous fish species. Sharks and rays are cartilaginous fish. There are about 200 types of rays and 370 types of sharks. Rays are flattened sharks. They live on the ocean floor. The manta ray, pictured here, is a cartilaginous fish.

Fish Features

All fish share some basic features. They are cold-blooded animals. This means they cannot control their body temperature. All fish have a sense of smell, too. Still, fish come in many shapes and sizes. Some have long, slim bodies. Others are flat or round.

Most fish have **streamlined** bodies. Fish have rounded heads. Their bodies narrow at the rear. Their necks blend into their bodies, too. This helps fish move quickly through the water. The barracuda has a streamlined body. It can swim at speeds of 36 miles (58 kilometers) per hour.

The barracuda is nicknamed "Tiger of the Sea."

Some lungfish breathe under water. Others rise to the water's surface to breathe.

Most fish have fins. Fish use their fins for swimming. Pectoral fins are on each side of the fish behind its head. Pelvic fins are behind the pectoral fins. They help the fish stop and steer. Many fish also have **dorsal** fins on their backs and **anal** fins on their undersides. Fish have a **caudal** fin on their tails. This fin steers and pushes the fish through the water.

Most fish fins do not have bones.

Most jawed fish have scales. Scales protect fish from **predators**. Mucus covers the skin and scales on bony fish. Mucus is a slippery substance that coats and protects parts of the body. Mucus makes fish skin feel slimy. Cartilaginous fish do not have mucus. Instead, they have an armor called denticles. Denticles feel like sandpaper.

Fast Facts

Lungfish do not have gills. They breathe through lungs.

Fish have an organ called the lateral line. This organ allows fish to feel an object before they see it.

Nearly all fish breathe through gills. Fish gulp water through their mouths. The water passes through the gills. The gills absorb, or take in, **oxygen** from the water.

First Fish

Scientists use **fossils** to learn about animal history. Scientists have found many sea animal fossils. They use these fossils to learn where fish came from.

Fish **ancestors** lived 500 million years ago. These sea animals were called sea squirts. Young sea squirts looked like fish. They were jawless. They had armor plates and scales to protect against predators. Sea squirts were the first animals with backbones. Many scientists believe they are the ancestors of all other animals with backbones.

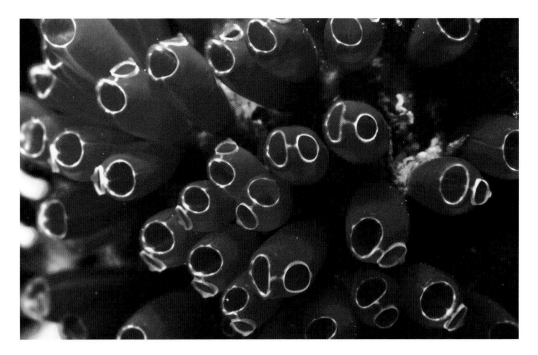

Adult sea squirts live on the sides of rocks or boats. They pump water in one hole and out another.

Many types of fish developed during the Devonian Period. This is known as the Age of Fish. The Devonian Period began about 400 million years ago. It ended 60 million years later. Hagfish, lampreys, cartilaginous fish, and bony fish developed during this time.

In 1998, scientists found a new coelacanth population off Sulawesi, Indonesia.

Fast Facts

The first coelacanth lived more than 350 million years ago. It has not changed much over time. Scientists once believed the coelacanth no longer lived any place on Earth. This fish was found in Africa's coastal waters in 1938.

The first modern fish were called *teleosts*. Teleosts developed about 225 million years ago.

About 200 to 300 new fish species are found each year.

Ray fossils are very rare.

Life Cycle

Lemon cichlids often
lay eggs in caves.

All fish begin life as eggs. Some fish produce many eggs at one time. Female cod lay up to 9 million eggs at one time. Other fish produce only a few eggs. Sharks lay only seven or eight eggs at one time.

All female fish produce eggs. Most fish lay eggs. Often, the male fish **fertilizes** the eggs as the female releases them from her body. Female tuna produce 50,000 eggs per pound (22,500 eggs per kilogram) of body weight. Fertilized eggs begin hatching after about 30 hours. The young tuna are called fry. Fry are only 0.1 inch (0.25 centimeters) long. Parents do not raise their fry. Many fry do not reach adulthood. Often, predators eat them. Bluefin tuna are adults when they reach about 8 years old. They live about 40 years.

Some male fish fertilize the eggs inside the female's body. Then, the female gives birth to live young. Guppies **reproduce** this way. Female guppies produce 20 to 100 live young. Adult guppies sometimes eat their young. Guppies are adults when they are between 3 and 6 months old.

Female sea horses lay their eggs in a pouch on the male's body.

Fish Flats

Fish live in all types of water. Some live in desert hot springs. Others live in cool mountain streams. About 40 percent of fish live in fresh water. Only 13 percent of fish live in the open ocean. Each fish species has a certain temperature in which it can live.

Eels live in shallow coastal waters throughout the world.

Fish live in many environments, too. Some fish live only in fresh water. Rivers, lakes, and streams are fresh water. Other fish live only in salt water. Oceans are salt water. There are some fish that can live in both fresh water and salt water. Eels are born in salt water. Still, they live most of their lives in fresh water.

The bald notothen's silvery color helps it blend in with the icy waters of Antarctica.

The bald notothen is found in antarctic water. This fish lives beneath the surface of the ice. Often, the bald notothen burrows inside the ice. These fish have **antifreeze** proteins. These proteins keep the fish from freezing in the cold waters. Many fish from tropical or moderate climates do not have antifreeze proteins.

Most tropical fish live in seagrass beds, coral reefs, rocks, and sand. Jacks, trevallys, sprats, and fusiliers are tropical fish.

Desert pupfish are found in the hot springs of western North America. They live in temperatures higher than 100° Fahrenheit (38° Celsius).

Tropical fish live in the waters of Africa, South and Central America, India, and Southeast Asia.

Fast Facts

The desert pupfish lives in desert springs or streams. Desert pupfish must burrow into the mud and remain still when the water becomes cooler in the winter.

Brotulids hold the record for the deepest dwelling fish. They live more than 23,000 feet (7,000 m) below the surface of the water.

Fish Food

Most fish are carnivores. This means they are meat-eating animals. Some eat shellfish. Others eat worms. Many fish eat other fish. These fish may even eat their own young. Angelfish often eat their own eggs and fry. Some fish do not eat other fish. They eat plants such as algae.

Many fish eat very small plants and animals called plankton. Humans cannot see plankton because they are so small. Fish use their mouths to suck in floating plankton. Whale sharks, giant manta rays, and basking sharks eat plankton.

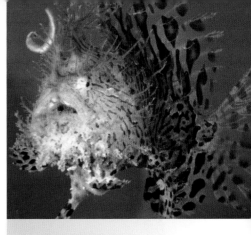

Anglerfish live deep in the ocean.

Some fish do not hunt for food. Instead, they hide in the rocks and coral. When another fish swims nearby, they open their mouths and swallow the fish. Anglerfish hide in the seabed. Their skin is camouflaged. This means it blends in with the environment. An anglerfish twitches its dorsal fin to attract other fish. The anglerfish pounces on its **prey**.

Fast Facts

Piranhas live in the Amazon River. They have razor-sharp teeth. Piranhas eat just about anything. They eat other fish, jaguars, cattle, and even humans.

Swordfish use their swordlike nose to hunt. A swordfish swims into a school of fish. The swordfish swings its sword to kill its prey.

Only about four piranha species are dangerous.

Mako sharks eat schooling fish including tuna, mackerel, swordfish, herring, and porpoise.

Threatened Fish

Animals that are in danger of becoming **extinct** are called endangered. This means that there are so few of the species that they need protection in order to survive. People are not allowed to hunt endangered animals in the United States.

There are many endangered fish species. In some cases, their habitat has become too **polluted** and unhealthy. Humans are destroying many fish habitats. Garbage is polluting the waters and some coral reefs. Pollutants increase **nitrogen** levels in water. This causes large amounts of algae to grow.

When air pollution mixes with rain it is called acid rain. Acid rain may kill fish and plants.

The algae blocks the sunlight the coral reef needs to survive. Many fish live in coral reefs. These fish have no place to live if the reef dies.

The Mekong Fish Conservation Project helps protect the Thailand giant catfish from becoming extinct.

The great white shark has been endangered in Australia since 1997.

Some fish have been overfished. This means humans have hunted more fish than are available to keep the species alive. Many shark species are at risk of becoming endangered.

Sharks are fished for their body parts. Shark fins are used to make shark fin soup. Other parts, such as livers and meat, are sold for food or health and beauty aid ingredients.

Fast Facts

The Thailand giant catfish is the largest freshwater fish in the world. It was declared endangered on June 2, 1970. This fish lives in the Mekong River in Thailand. The population of this fish has dropped from 256 to 96 since a hydroelectric dam was built on the river in 1994. A dam is a structure used to block water.

Scientists believe the Chinook salmon may become extinct by 2016.

Activities

Shoebox Fish Habitat

Fish live in all types of environments. The following activity shows how to create a fish habitat inside a shoebox.

Materials

- craft paper
- magazines with pictures of fish
- shoebox
- crayons or markers
- tape

- thread
- scissors
- pipe cleaners
- glitter
- glue

1. Decorate the inside of the box. Make it look like an underwater habitat. Use pipe cleaners to make coral. Glitter can be used to make bubbles. Use green craft paper to make seaweed. Draw the water, rocks, seaweed, and fish. You can even draw scuba divers and submarines.

2. Draw pictures of fish. Cut out the pictures. You can cut out pictures of fish from magazines, too.

3. Glue the fish to craft paper so they do not bend.

4. Hang the fish inside the shoebox using the tape and thread.

Anenomefish protect anenomes. In return, the anenome give the fish a shelter where they can lay their eggs.

Water Bodies

Fish have streamlined bodies. This helps them move quickly through the water. The following activity shows why the shape of a fish's body is important.

Materials

- modeling clay
- pipe cleaners
- wire clothes hanger
- tub with about 6 inches (15 cm) of cool water

1. Divide the clay into two pieces.
2. Make a flat cube from one piece of clay.
3. Make a slim, smooth, streamlined shape from the other piece of clay.
4. Place a pipe cleaner in the center of each piece of clay.
5. Loosely hang the pipe cleaners and clay from the wire hanger. Make sure both pipe cleaners swing freely from the hanger. The clay should hang about 8 inches (20 cm) from the hanger.
6. Hold the top of the hanger, and place the clay in the tub of water.
7. Slowly pull the hanger in a straight line across the water. Pretend you are racing the two clay pieces.
8. Which piece of clay moved more quickly through the water? Why?

About 200 to 300 new fish species are discovered each year.

Quiz

What have you learned about fish? See if you can answer the following questions correctly.

1. What were the first fish called?

2. Where do fish live?

3. How do fish breathe?

4. What do fish eat?

5. How do fish move through water?

After a few days of living in one place, a Commerson's frogfish can change color to blend in with its environment.

Answers: 1. The first fish were called sea squirts. 2. Fish live in all types of water. Fish live in fresh water or salt water. 3. Most fish breathe using gills. 4. Most fish are meat-eating animals. Some eat shellfish. Others eat worms. Most fish eat other fish. Some fish eat plants such as algae. 5. Fish have streamlined bodies. They use their fins to move through water.

Further Reading

Parker, Steve, Dave King (photographer), and Colin Keates (photographer). *Eyewitness: Fish*. New York, NY: DK Publishing, 2003.

Walker, Sally M. *Fossil Fish Found Alive: Discovering the Coelacanth*. Minneapolis, MN: Carolrhoda Books, 2002.

Woods, Samuel G. *The Amazing Book of Fish Records and Other Ocean Creatures: The Largest, the Smallest, the Fastest, and Many More*. Blackbirch Marketing, 2000.

Web Sites

For more fish information, visit the Florida Museum of Natural History Just for Kids page at www.flmnh.ufl.edu/fish/Kids/kids.htm

Detailed information about the coelacanth is available at www.dinofish.com

Leafy seadragons have leaflike parts that make these fish look like seaweed.

Glossary

anal near the back or underside

ancestors animals from the past that are related to modern animals

antifreeze a substance that lowers the freezing point of a liquid

caudal near the tail or hind parts

dorsal near the back or upper surface

extinct no longer living

fertilizes makes another animal able to produce young

fossils rocklike remains of ancient animals or plants

habitats places where animals live in nature

nitrogen a gas with no color or smell that is found in all living things

oxygen a gas with no color or smell that animals and plants need to live

polluted made unfit or harmful

predators animals that eat the flesh of other animals

prey animals that are hunted for food

reproduce to produce young

species type or sort

streamlined designed to move easily through water or air

Index